ACCELERATED

PIANO

Adventures® *by Nancy and Randall Faber*

_____ is sightreading this book!
(your name)

Production Coordinator: Jon Ophoff
Cover and Illustrations: Terpstra Design, San Francisco

ISBN 978-1-61677-659-6
Copyright © 2014 Dovetree Productions, Inc.
c/o FABER PIANO ADVENTURES, 3042 Creek Dr., Ann Arbor, MI 48108.
International Copyright Secured. All Rights Reserved. Printed in U.S.A.
WARNING: The music, text, design, and graphics in this publication are protected
by copyright law. Any duplication is an infringement of U.S. copyright law.

CHART YOUR PROGRESS

Sightreading for Lesson Book 1, p. 19
My Invention...................................... **6-8**

DAY 1   DAY 2   DAY 3   DAY 4   DAY 5

Sightreading for Lesson Book 1, p. 37
French Minuet **30-32**

DAY 1   DAY 2   DAY 3   DAY 4   DAY 5

Sightreading for Lesson Book 1, pp. 22-23
Roman Trumpets **9-11**

DAY 1   DAY 2   DAY 3   DAY 4   DAY 5

Sightreading for Lesson Book 1, pp. 38-39
Morning **33-35**

DAY 1   DAY 2   DAY 3   DAY 4   DAY 5

Sightreading for Lesson Book 1, p. 25
Chant of the Monks **12-14**

DAY 1   DAY 2   DAY 3   DAY 4   DAY 5

Sightreading for Lesson Book 1, pp. 40-41
Oh! Susanna **36-38**

DAY 1   DAY 2   DAY 3   DAY 4   DAY 5

Sightreading for Lesson Book 1, p. 27
Minuet **15-17**

DAY 1   DAY 2   DAY 3   DAY 4   DAY 5

Sightreading for Lesson Book 1, pp. 44-45
Ode to Joy **39-41**

DAY 1   DAY 2   DAY 3   DAY 4   DAY 5

Sightreading for Lesson Book 1, p. 28
Russian Folk Song **18-20**

DAY 1   DAY 2   DAY 3   DAY 4   DAY 5

Sightreading for Lesson Book 1, p. 47
Hungarian Dance **42-44**

DAY 1   DAY 2   DAY 3   DAY 4   DAY 5

Sightreading for Lesson Book 1, p. 30
Bus Stop Boogie.......................... **21-23**

DAY 1   DAY 2   DAY 3   DAY 4   DAY 5

Sightreading for Lesson Book 1, p. 49
Waltz **45-47**

DAY 1   DAY 2   DAY 3   DAY 4   DAY 5

Sightreading for Lesson Book 1, pp. 32-33
Eine Kleine Nachtmusik.............. **24-26**

DAY 1   DAY 2   DAY 3   DAY 4   DAY 5

Sightreading for Lesson Book 1, p. 51
Halftime Show **48-50**

DAY 1   DAY 2   DAY 3   DAY 4   DAY 5

Sightreading for Lesson Book 1, pp. 34-35
Gypsy Band.................................. **27-29**

DAY 1   DAY 2   DAY 3   DAY 4   DAY 5

Sightreading for Lesson Book 1, pp. 52-53
Racecar Rally **51-53**

DAY 1   DAY 2   DAY 3   DAY 4   DAY 5

SIGHTREADING SKILL

Sightreading skill is a powerful asset for the developing musician. It makes every step of music-making easier. With the right tools and a little effort, sightreading skill can be developed to great benefit.

This book builds confident readers in two ways:

1. Recognition of **individual notes**, and
2. Perception of **note patterns**, both rhythmic and melodic

In language literacy, the reader must not only identify single words, but also group words together for understanding. Similarly, music reading involves more than note naming. The sightreader tracks *horizontally* and *vertically*, observing intervals and contour while gleaning familiar patterns that make up the musical context.

This decoding skill requires repetition within familiar musical contexts. In other words, pattern recognition develops by seeing a lot of the same patterns. Accordingly, this book presents **musical variations** to sharpen perception of the *new* against a backdrop of the *familiar*. To use the literacy analogy, the musician must not only identify single notes, but also group notes into musical patterns for understanding.

In the Accelerated Sightreading Book 1, these musical variations are drawn from the classical music introduced in the Lesson Book—Bach, Beethoven, Borodin, Brahms, Grieg, Haydn, Mozart, Rameau—as well as traditional folk songs from around the world.

Students will sightread music which uses the following concepts: eighth note rhythms, all the notes of the grand staff, intervals of a 2nd, 3rd, 4th, 5th, and octave, C and G five-finger scale melodies, and I and V7 chords in the keys of C and G.

SIGHTREADING

How to Use

This book is organized into sets of 5 exercises, for 5 days of practice. Each set provides variations on a piece from the Piano Adventures® Accelerated Lesson Book 1. Play one exercise a day, completing one set per week.

Though the student is not required to repeatedly "practice" the sightreading exercise, each should be repeated once or twice as indicated by the repeat sign. For an extra workout, play each of the previous exercises in the set before playing the new exercise of the day.

Curiosity and Fun

The "Don't Practice This!" motto is a bold statement which has an obvious psychological impact. It reminds us that sightreading is indeed the first time through and it reminds us to keep the activity fun.

Level of Difficulty

It is most beneficial to sightread at the appropriate level of difficulty. Some experts say that a child should not stumble on more than three or four words per page when reading. Similarly, a music student should not stumble on more than three or four notes per page when sightreading. This Piano Adventures® Sightreading Book is carefully written to match an early level of difficulty for the older beginner, providing an appropriate degree of challenge.

Marking Progress

Students are encouraged to draw a large **X** over each completed exercise. This instruction is so out of the ordinary that students find it quite satisfying to mark their progress in this way.

Some students may exclaim about the thickness of the book! They soon are rewarded to find how fast they can move through it. Indeed, with confidence increasing, the student can take pride in moving to completion of this very large book ... and do so with a crescendo of achievement.

Instructions to the Student

1. **Always scan the music before playing.**
   First notice the time signature. Then silently count the first two to four measures.
   If there are 8th notes, subdivide the beat (1 + 2 +). Do you notice any rhythm patterns?

2. **Find the starting position for each hand.**
   Scan the music for skips, larger intervals, dynamic marks, sharps, flats, and rests.
   Also, scan the music for any hand shifts.

3. **Count-off.**
   Set a slow, steady tempo
   of two measures and begin
   to play. Keep your eyes
   moving ahead! Repeat the exercise,
   then cross it out.

DAY 1: My Invention

Notice the starting L.H. finger.

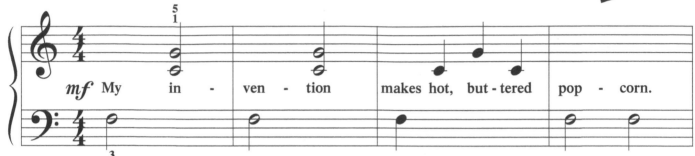

DAY 2: My Invention

Notice the starting L.H. finger.
Notice the change from *f* to *p* on the repeat.

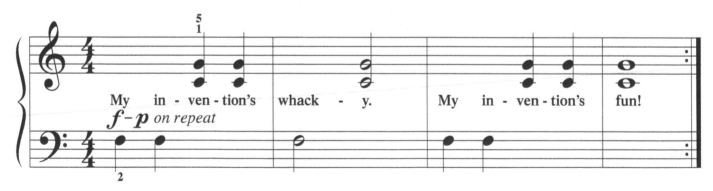

Name the 3 notes used in the music from bottom to top.

1. _____ 2. _____ 3. _____
   bottom   middle   top

DAY 3: My Invention

Notice the starting L.H. finger.

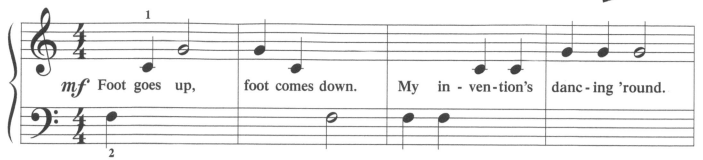

DAY 4: My Invention

Feel the 4 beats for each whole note!
Notice the L.H. finger changes at measure 3.

DAY 5: My Invention

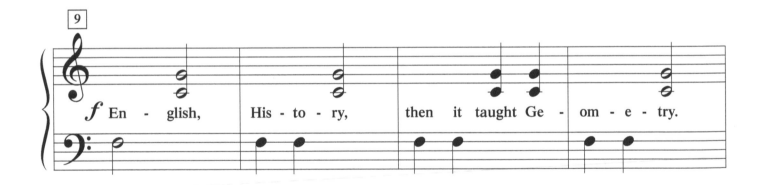

Name the notes used in measures 1-8.

DAY 1: Roman Trumpets

DON'T PRACTICE THIS!

Prepare the L.H. before starting.
Prepare your right foot on the damper pedal.

f Ro - man trum - pets   call - ing   in   the   big   cit - y   square. (2-3-4)

1 - 2,   1 - 2,   1 - 2 - 3 - 4,   Sound   eve - ry - where!

DAY 2: Roman Trumpets

Prepare the L.H. before starting.

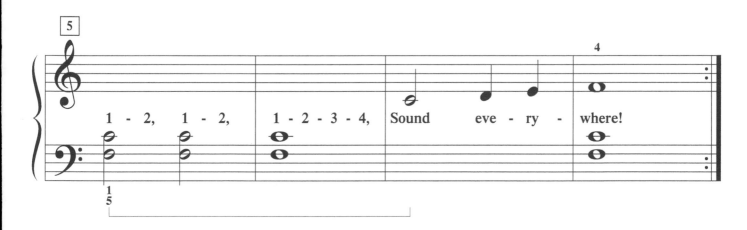

f Hear the gold - en   trum - pets.   Hear the gold - en   ech - o.
p

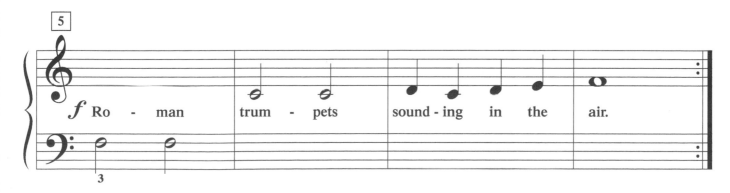

f Ro - man   trum - pets   sound - ing   in   the   air.

DAY 3: Roman Trumpets

Remember to prepare the L.H. before starting.

DAY 4: Roman Trumpets

Play with only finger 2s.
Notice the damper pedal is held down throughout the piece.

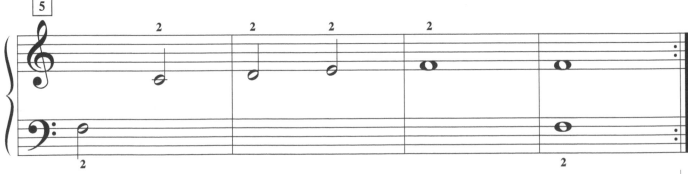

DAY 5: Roman Trumpets

Look silently through the piece.
Can you find a R.H. pattern before you sightread?

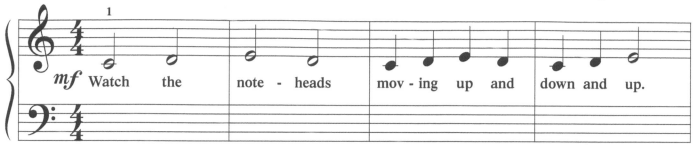

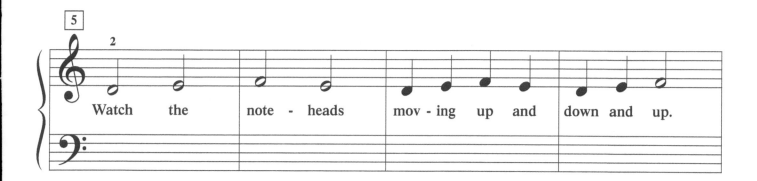

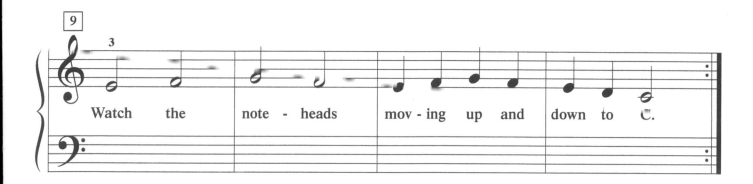

Name the notes.

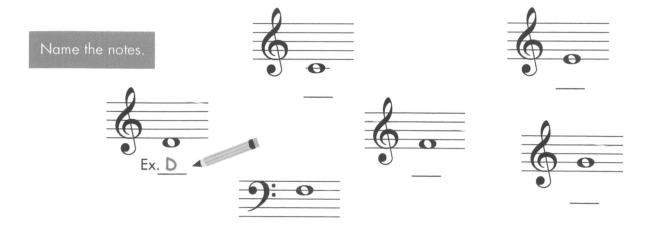

Ex. D

DAY 1: Chant of the Monks

Listen for a smooth legato.

Al - le - lu - ia, Al - le - lu - ia.

f - p on repeat

DAY 2: Chant of the Monks

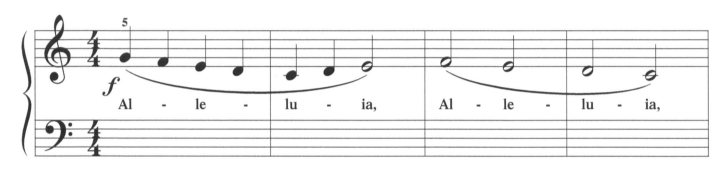

f

Al - le - lu - ia, Al - le - lu - ia,

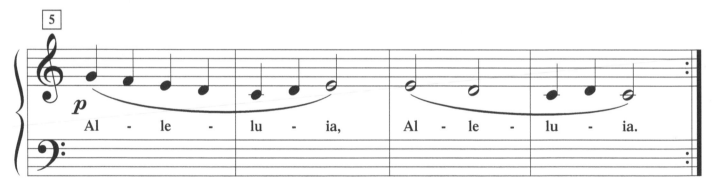

p

Al - le - lu - ia, Al - le - lu - ia.

> Now play DAY 2 hands-together. Your L.H. will play the same melody in a lower C scale. Watch for changes in note direction!

SIGHTREADING

DAY 3: Chant of the Monks

Notice the echo at measure 5.

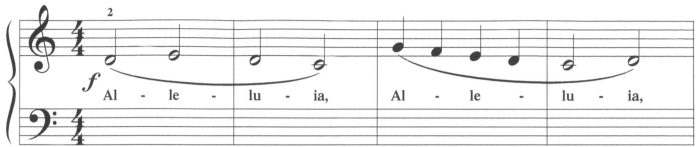

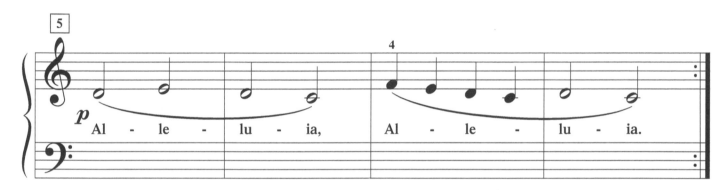

DAY 4: Chant of the Monks

Where does the dynamic mark change?

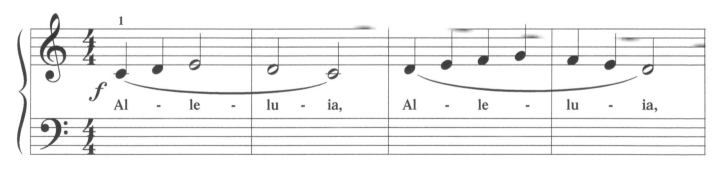

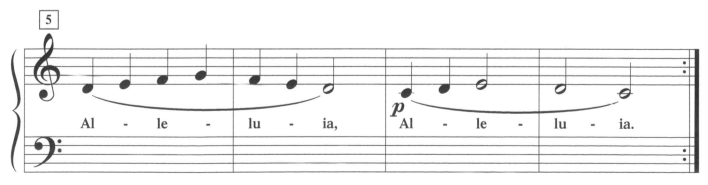

DAY 5: Chant of the Monks

Play first with R.H. alone. Repeat playing hands together!

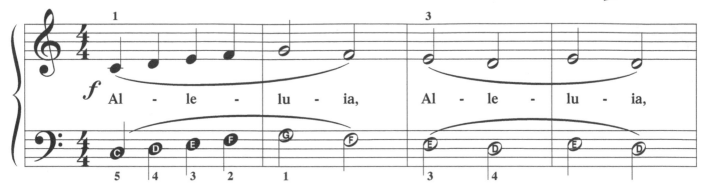

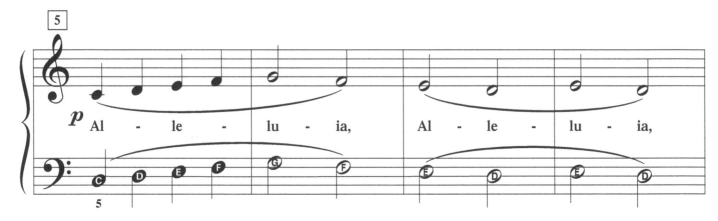

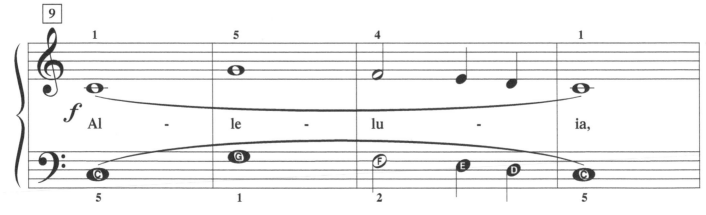

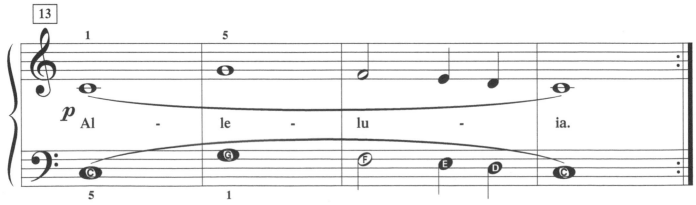

DAY 1: Minuet

Notice the new time signature.

DON'T PRACTICE THIS!

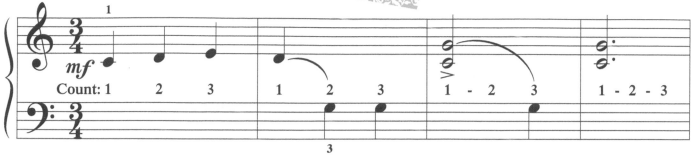

Count: 1   2   3   1   2   3   1 - 2   3   1 - 2 - 3

DAY 2: Minuet

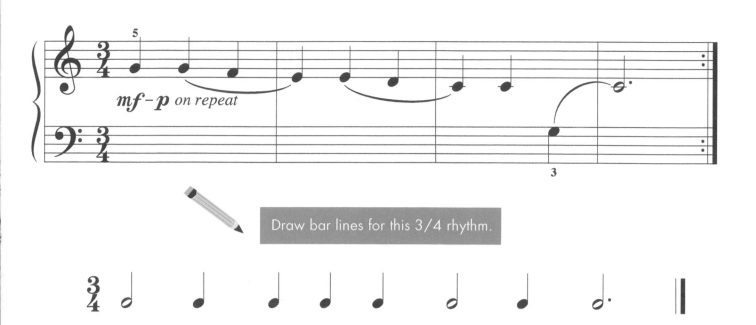

mf–p on repeat

Draw bar lines for this 3/4 rhythm.

15

DAY 3: Minuet

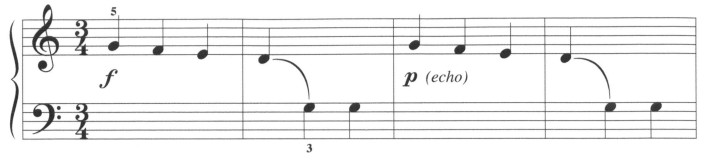

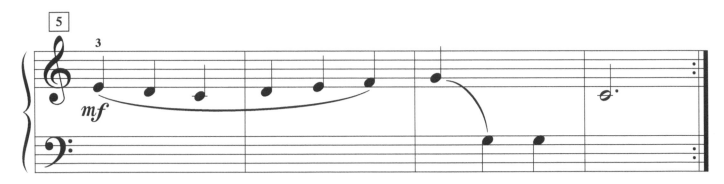

DAY 4: Minuet

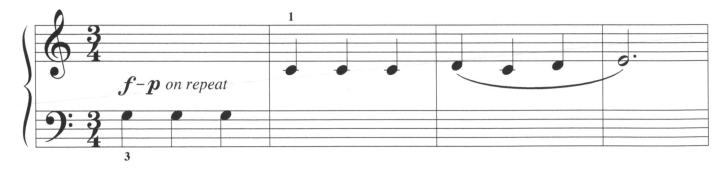

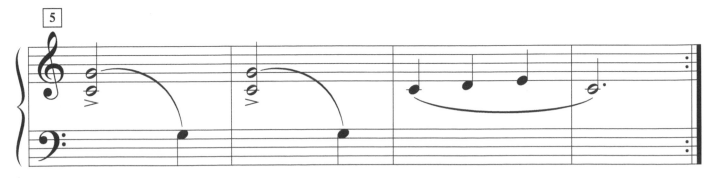

DAY 5: Minuet

DON'T PRACTICE THIS!

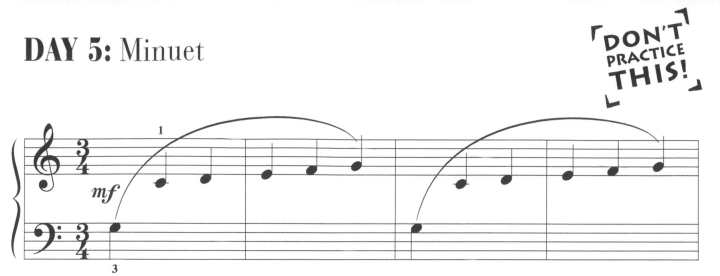

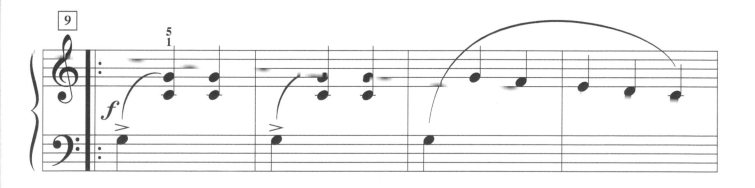

Repeat from measure 1.

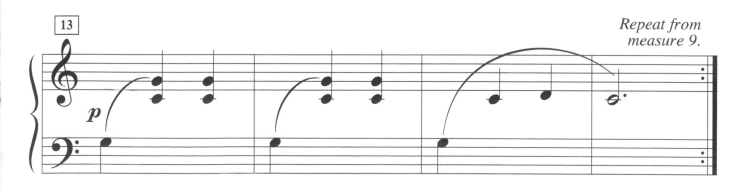

Repeat from measure 9.

DAY 1: Russian Folk Song

DAY 2: Russian Folk Song

Before starting, silently count the rhythm of measures 1-2.

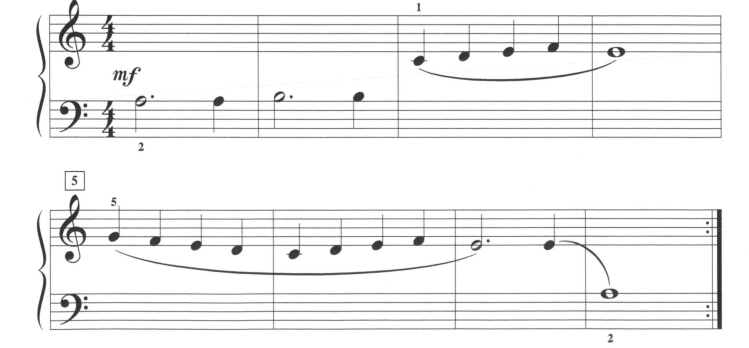

DAY 3: Russian Folk Song

Before starting, silently count the rhythm of measures 3-4.

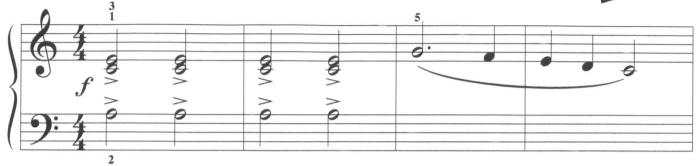

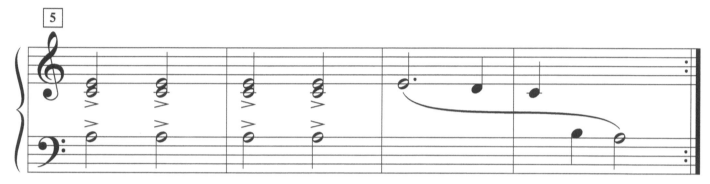

DAY 4: Russian Folk Song

Notice the notes begin softly and grow louder.

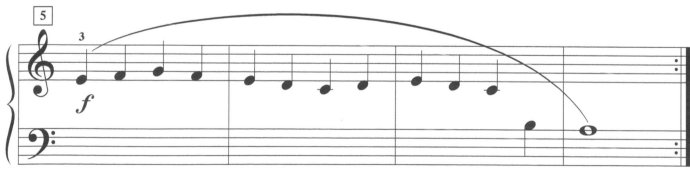

SIGHTREADING

based on Accel. Lesson Book 1, p. 28

DAY 5: Russian Folk Song

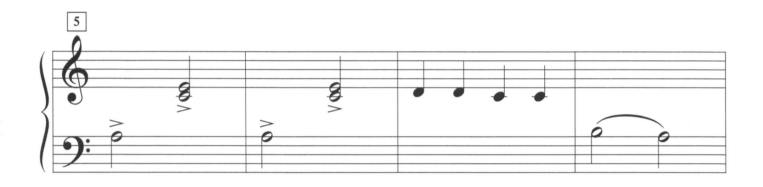

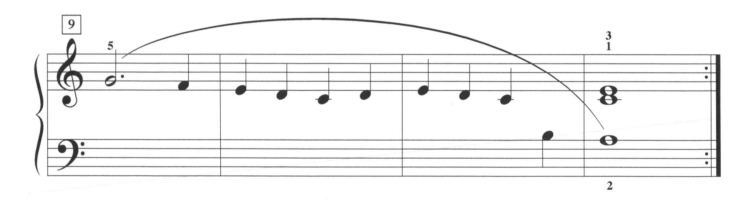

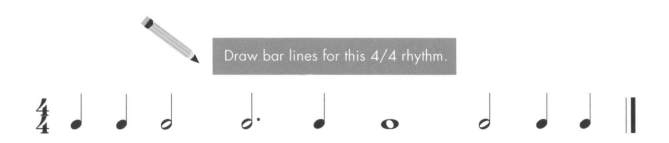

Draw bar lines for this 4/4 rhythm.

based on Accel. Lesson Book 1, p. 30

SIGHTREADING

DAY 1: Bus Stop Boogie

DON'T PRACTICE THIS!

Prepare the L.H. before starting.

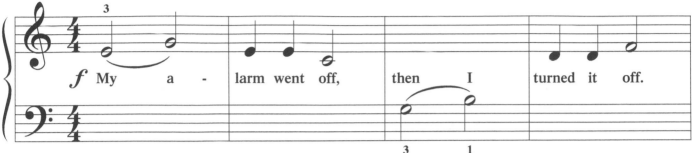

f My a - larm went off, then I turned it off.

When I turned it off I went back to sleep.

DAY 2: Bus Stop Boogie

Remember to prepare the L.H. before starting.
Watch for 3rds (skips)!

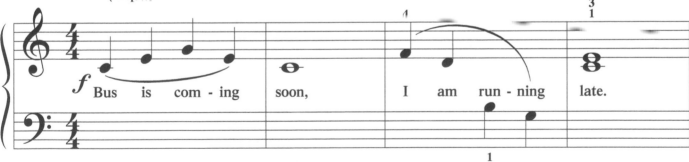

f Bus is com - ing soon, I am run - ning late.

p Can - not find my book, hope that it will wait!

DAY 3: Bus Stop Boogie

DON'T PRACTICE THIS!

Watch for 3rds (skips)!

DAY 4: Bus Stop Boogie

Compare the first and second lines. What do you notice?

DAY 5: Bus Stop Boogie

Notice this melody has many groups of repeated notes.

Draw a 3rd UP or DOWN from each note. Then name both notes.

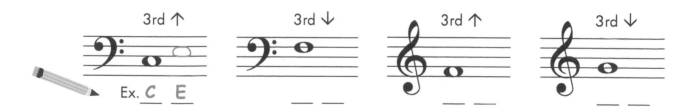

3rd ↑   3rd ↓   3rd ↑   3rd ↓

Ex. C E

DAY 1: Eine Kleine Nachtmusik

Prepare the L.H. before starting.

DON'T PRACTICE THIS!

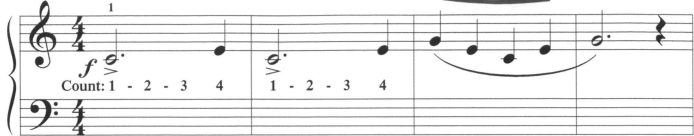

Count: 1 - 2 - 3   4   1 - 2 - 3   4

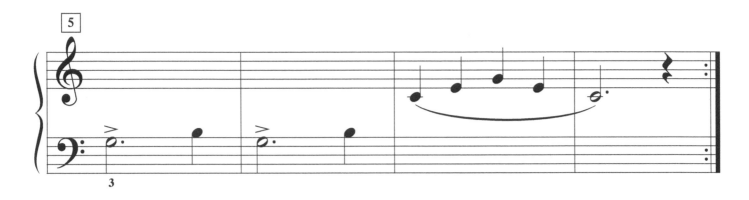

DAY 2: Eine Kleine Nachtmusik

Prepare the L.H. before starting.

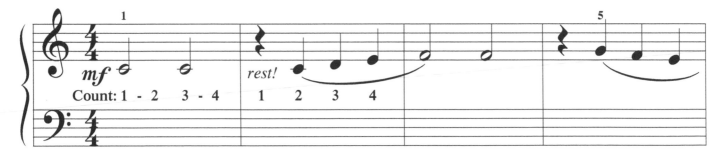

Count: 1 - 2   3 - 4   rest!   1   2   3   4

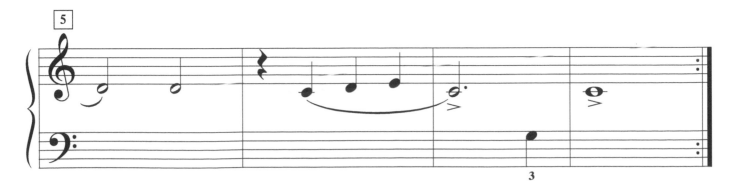

DON'T PRACTICE THIS!

DAY 3: Eine Kleine Nachtmusik

Before starting, silently count the rhythm of measures 1-2.
Prepare the L.H. before starting.

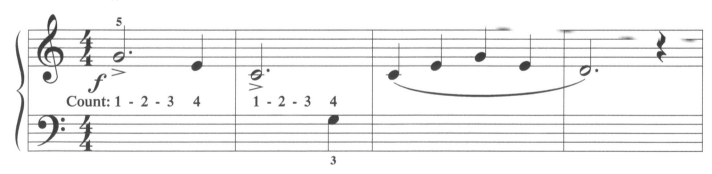

DAY 4: Eine Kleine Nachtmusik

Before starting, silently count the rhythm of measures 1-2.

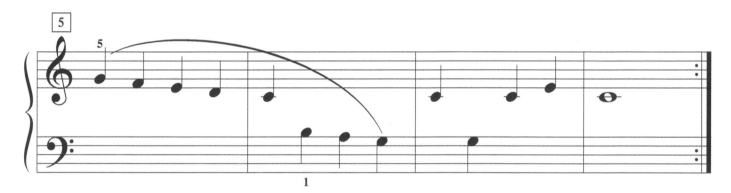

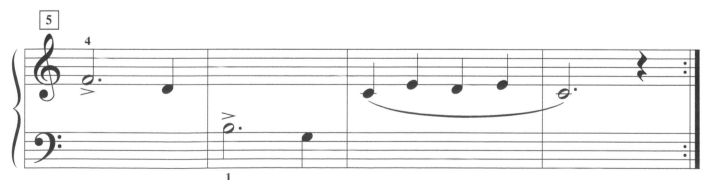

DAY 5: Eine Kleine Nachtmusik

DON'T PRACTICE THIS!

Draw bar lines for this 4/4 rhythm.

DAY 1: Gypsy Band

Be sure to hold the L.H. ties.

DAY 2: Gypsy Band

Prepare the L.H. before starting.

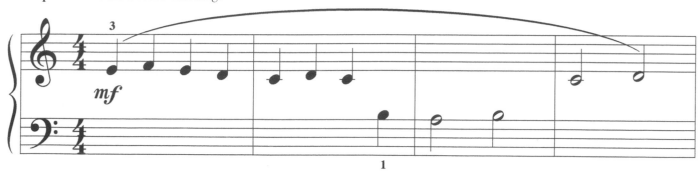

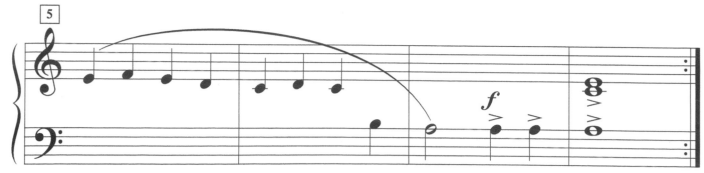

DAY 3: Gypsy Band

Do you see a rhythm pattern in the first line?

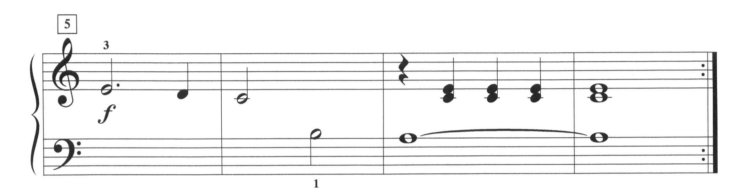

DAY 4: Gypsy Band

Do you see a rhythm pattern in the first line?

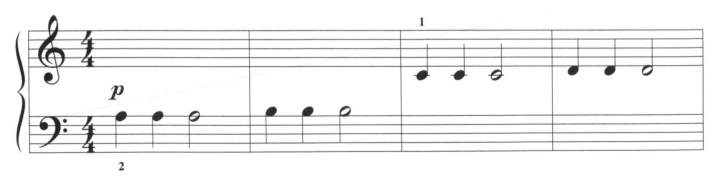

DAY 5: Gypsy Band

Use only finger 2s to play this song.

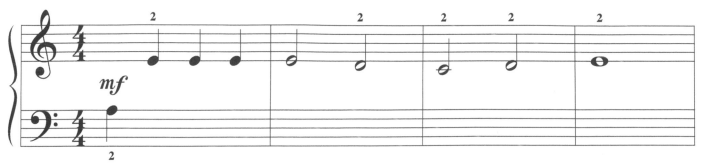

Write the total number of beats for each example.

beats   beats   beats   beats

29

DAY 1: French Minuet

Before starting, silently count
the rhythm of measures 1-2.

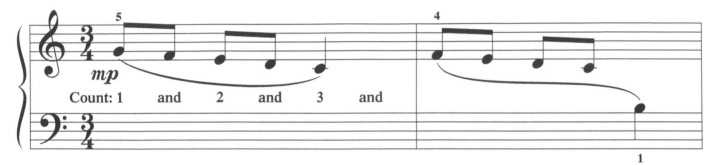

mp

Count: 1   and   2   and   3   and

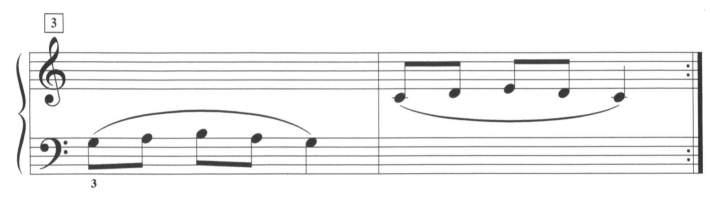

DAY 2: French Minuet

Before starting, silently count the rhythm of measures 1-2.

mp

Count: 1   and   2   and   3   and

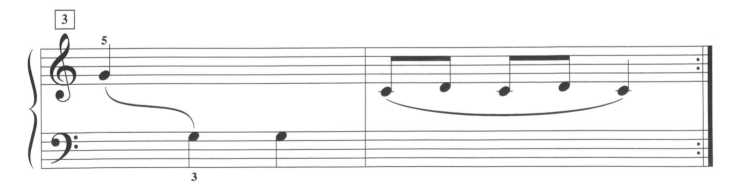

DAY 3: French Minuet

Before starting, silently count the rhythm of measures 1-2.

DAY 4: French Minuet

Before starting, silently count the rhythm of measures 1-2.

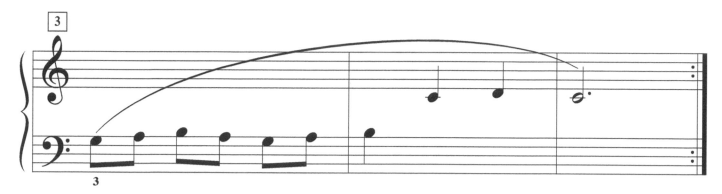

DAY 5: French Minuet

Before starting, silently count the rhythm of measures 1-2.

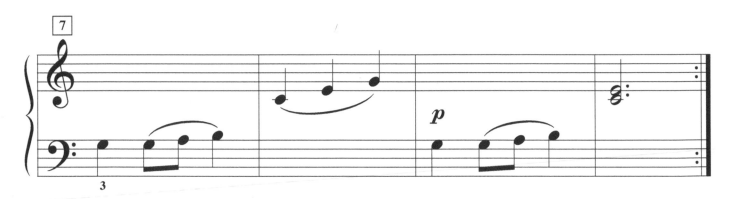

Draw bar lines for this 3/4 rhythm.

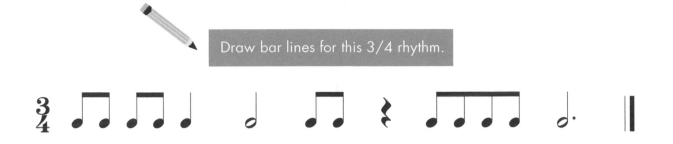

DAY 1: Morning

Remember, a phrase is a "musical sentence."

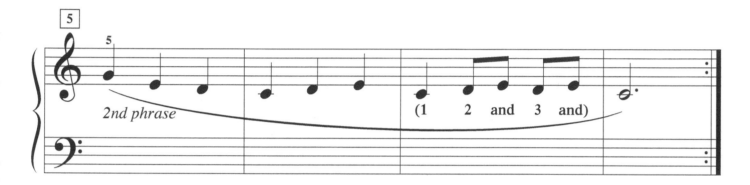

DAY 2: Morning

DAY 3: Morning

DON'T PRACTICE THIS!

DAY 4: Morning

DAY 5: Morning

Notice the tie within a slur at the end of the piece.

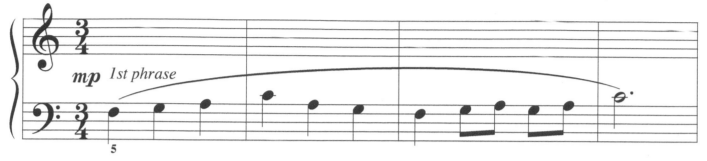

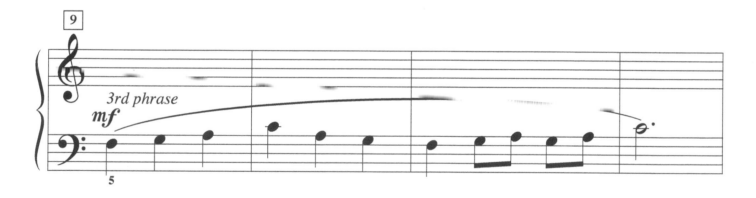

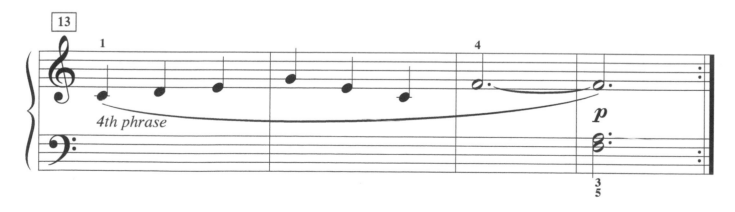

DAY 1: Oh! Susanna

This melody begins with pick-up notes.

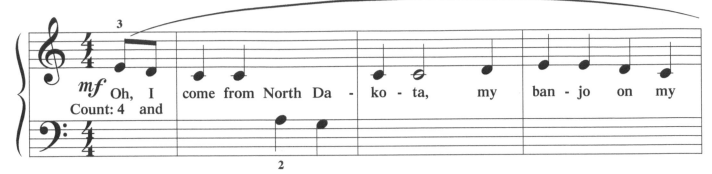

DAY 2: Oh! Susanna

Prepare the L.H. before starting.

DAY 3: Oh! Susanna

On what beat do you begin?

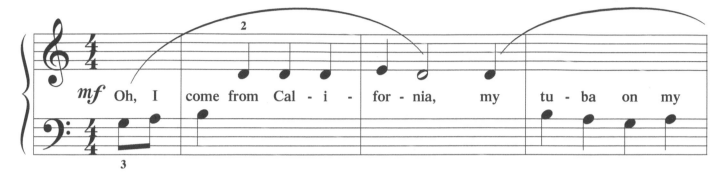

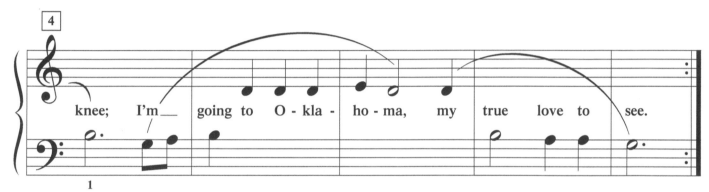

DAY 4: Oh! Susanna

On what beat do you begin?

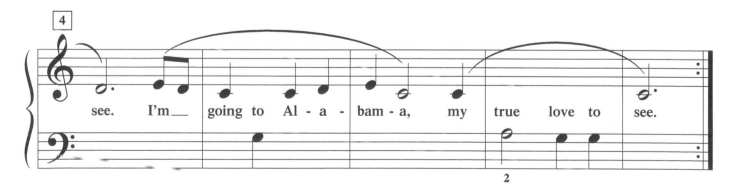

DAY 5: Oh! Susanna

DON'T PRACTICE THIS!

Oh! Su - san - na, don't you cry for me; 'cuz if you

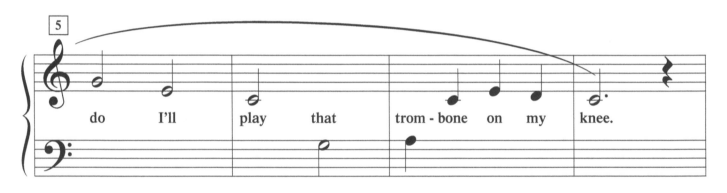

do I'll play that trom - bone on my knee.

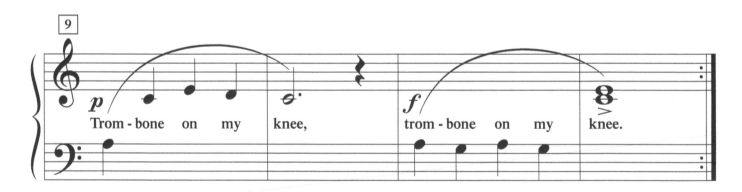

Trom - bone on my knee, trom - bone on my knee.

Make up your own rhythm in 4/4 time!

pick-up   measure   measure   measure

DAY 1: Ode to Joy

_____ **5-Finger Scale**

Plan how you will play the 8th notes.

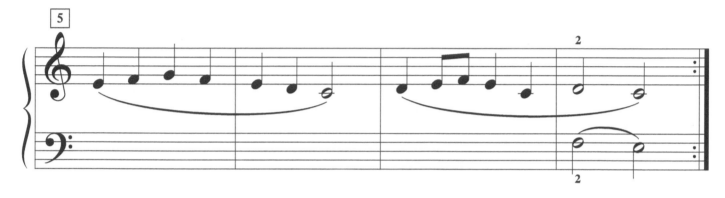

DAY 2: Ode to Joy

_____ **5-Finger Scale**
(for L.H. alone)

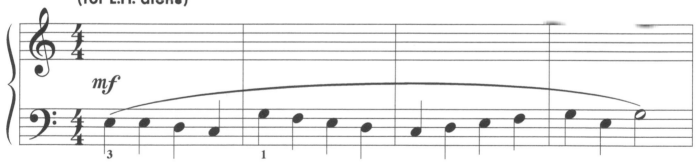

DAY 3: Ode to Joy

_____ 5-Finger Scale

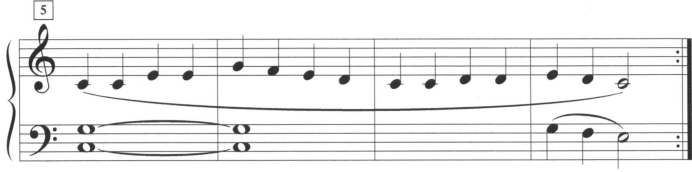

DAY 4: Ode to Joy

_____ 5-Finger Scale

Notice in measure 3 the music becomes louder.

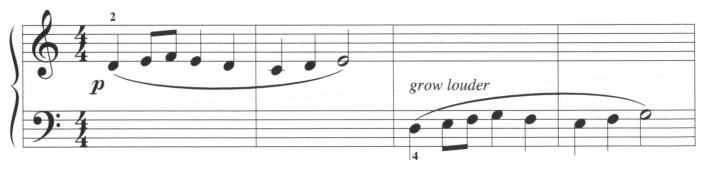

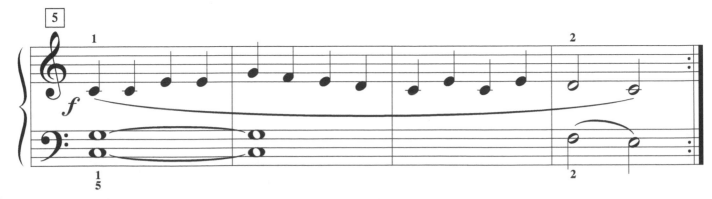

DAY 5: Ode to Joy

_____ **5-Finger Scale**

DON'T
PRACTICE
THIS!

How do the L.H. notes relate to the R.H. notes?

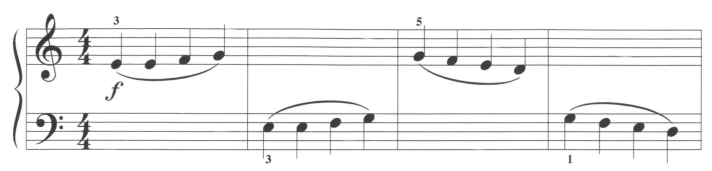

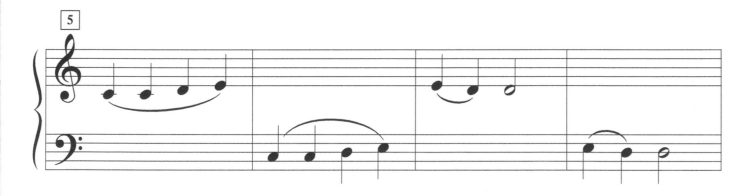

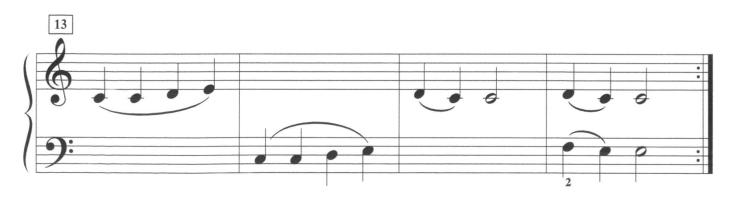

DAY 1: Hungarian Dance
_____ 5-Finger Scale

DAY 2: Hungarian Dance
_____ 5-Finger Scale

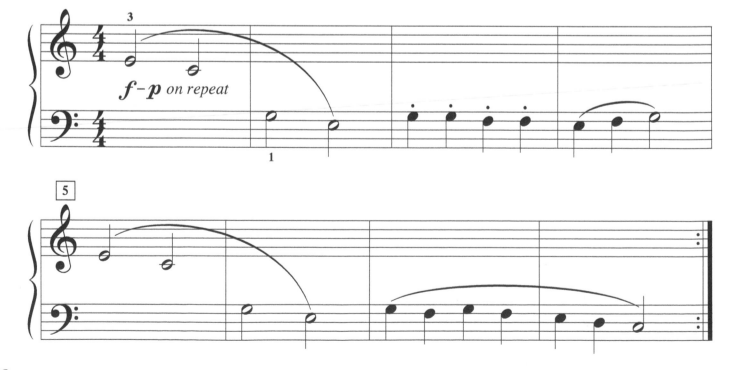

DAY 3: Hungarian Dance

_____ 5-Finger Scale

f - p on repeat

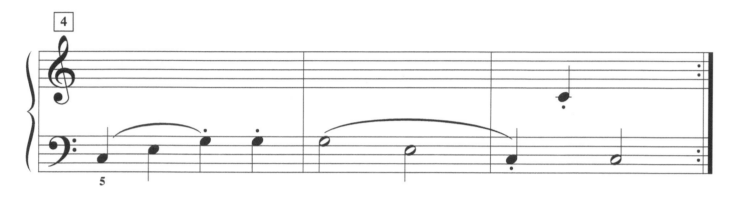

DAY 4: Hungarian Dance

_____ 5-Finger Scale

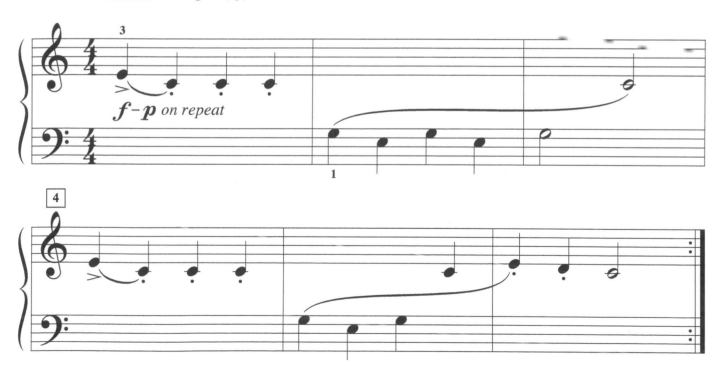

f - p on repeat

43

SIGHTREADING

based on Accel. Lesson Book 1, p. 47

DAY 5: Hungarian Dance

_____ 5-Finger Scale

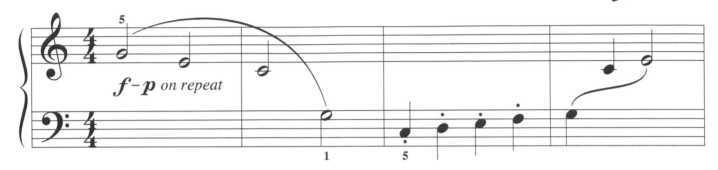

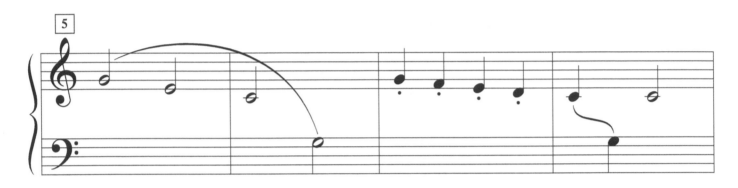

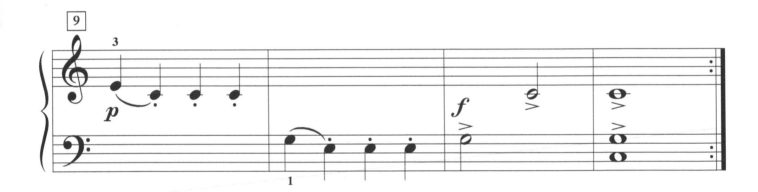

Put an X through the incorrect measures in 4/4 time.

DAY 1: Waltz

Plan how you will play the R.H. shifts.

DON'T PRACTICE THIS!

DAY 2: Waltz

Notice the R.H. starting position.

DAY 3: Waltz

Notice the R.H. starting position.
Prepare the L.H. final notes.

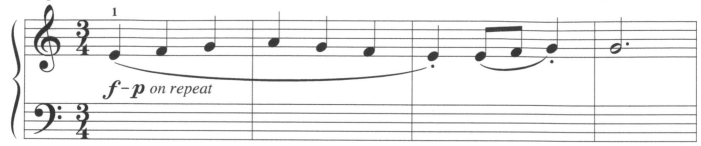

f–p on repeat

DAY 4: Waltz

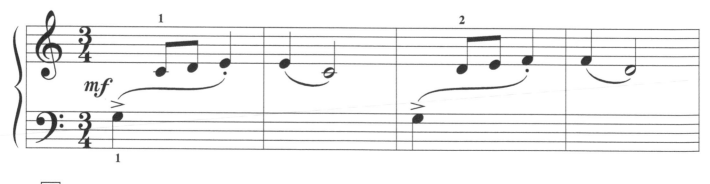

mf

DAY 5: Waltz

Notice the L.H. and R.H. starting positions.

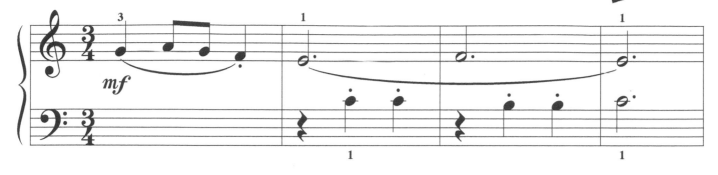

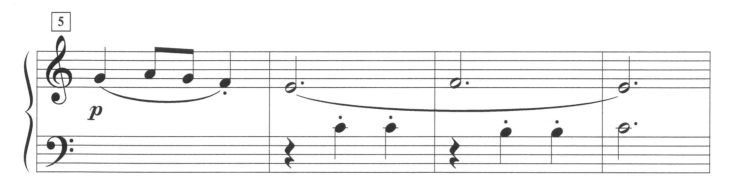

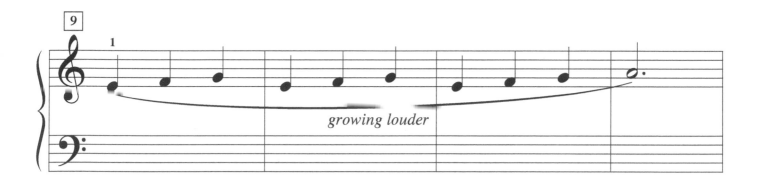

growing louder

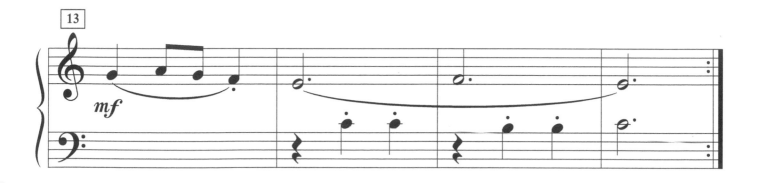

DAY 1: Halftime Show

Notice the new 2/4 time signature.

Count: 1 + 2 + 1 + 2 +

Our band is so strong, play - ing our fight song.

5
Rah, rah, rah, rah! Cheer for our school band!

DAY 2: Halftime Show

Count: 1 + 2 + 1 + 2 +

Watch the trum - pets blow. What a half - time show!

5
Drums go rat - a - tat. What a half - time show!

DAY 3: Halftime Show

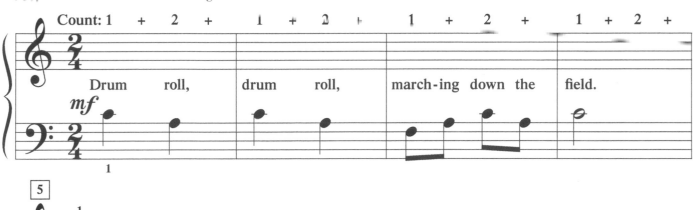

DAY 4: Halftime Show

Prepare the R.H. before starting.

DAY 5: Halftime Show

Notice the R.H. starting note.
Does this melody move in 2nds or 3rds?

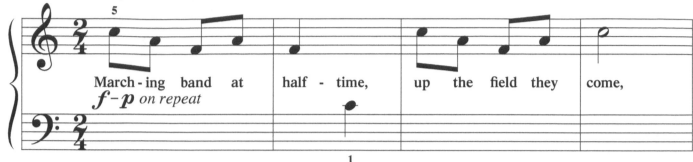

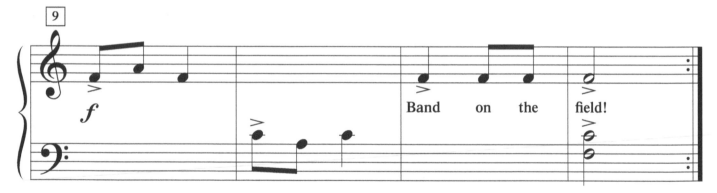

Practice naming these notes aloud as fast as you can.

DAY 1: Racecar Rally

Plan how you will play the rhythm of measures 1-2.

Check-ered flags wave____ and the race be - gins!

All of the driv - ers would like to win.

DAY 2: Racecar Rally

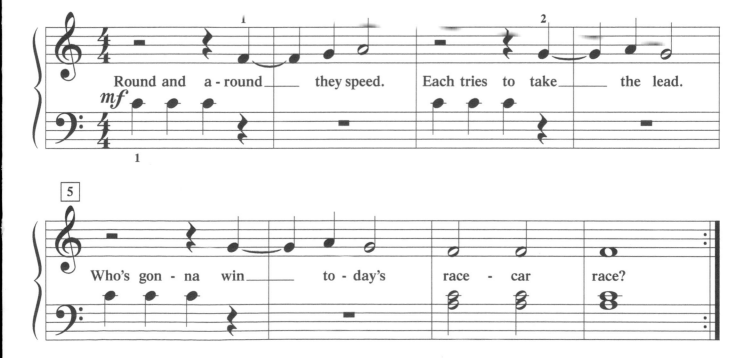

Round and a-round____ they speed. Each tries to take____ the lead.

Who's gon - na win____ to - day's race - car race?

DAY 3: Racecar Rally

DON'T
PRACTICE
THIS!

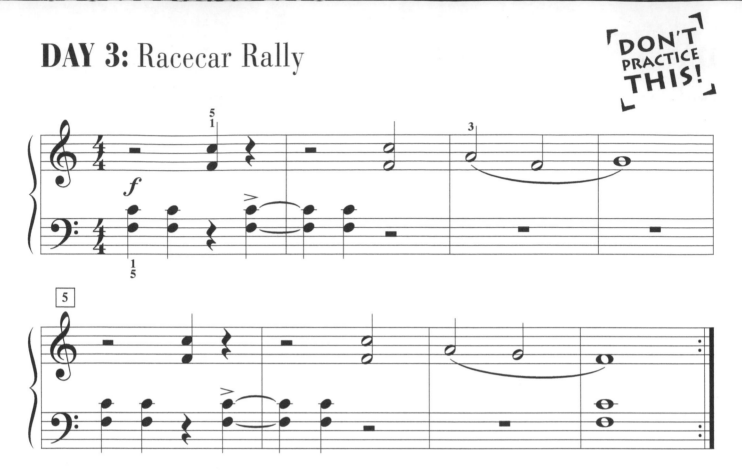

DAY 4: Racecar Rally

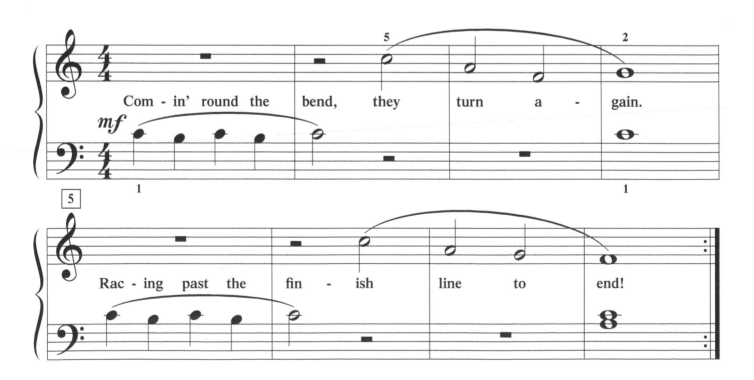

Com - in' round the bend, they turn a - gain.

Rac - ing past the fin - ish line to end!

DAY 5: Racecar Rally

DAY 1: English Minuet

Notice in measure 7 the same fingers play together.

DON'T PRACTICE THIS!

DAY 2: English Minuet

Plan how you will count the rhythm of measures 1-2.

DAY 3: English Minuet

Prepare the R.H. before starting.

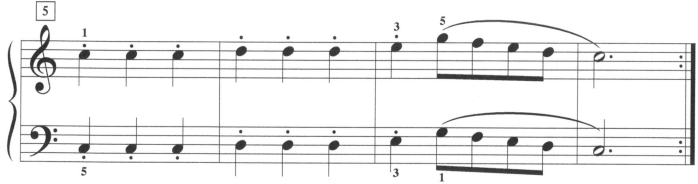

DAY 4: English Minuet

DAY 5: English Minuet

Plan the L.H. octave leap at the end.

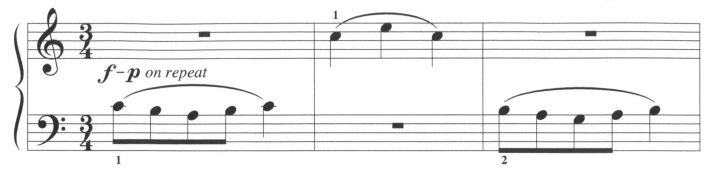

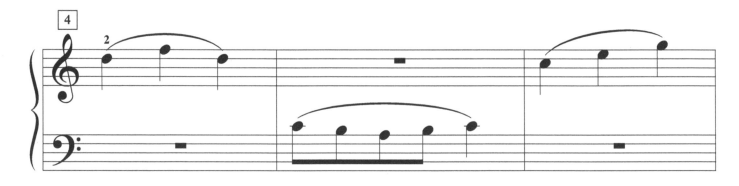

Practice naming these notes aloud as fast as you can.

DAY 1: Two-Hand Conversation

Find the imitation before sightreading.

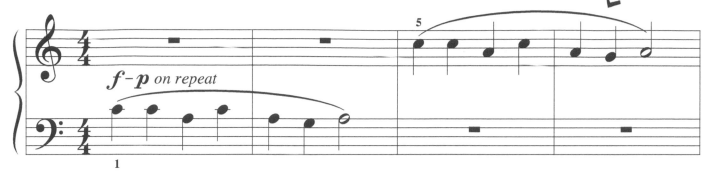

DAY 2: Two-Hand Conversation

Does the R.H. imitate the L.H.?

DAY 3: Two-Hand Conversation

Plan how you will play the octave leap at the end.

DAY 4: Two-Hand Conversation

Plan how you will play the rhythm in measure 1.

DAY 5: Two-Hand Conversation

DON'T PRACTICE THIS!

Does the opening rhythm pattern continue throughout the piece?

Count: 1   +   2   3   +   4

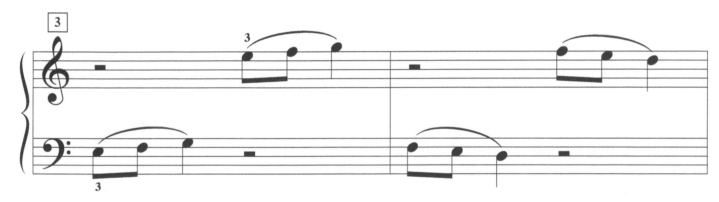

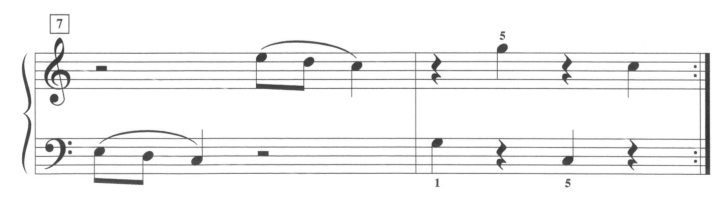

DAY 1: When the Saints Go Marching In

This melody begins with pick-up notes. Notice you begin on beat 2.

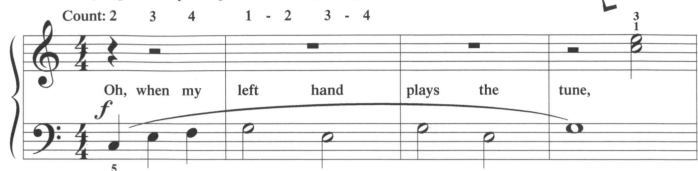

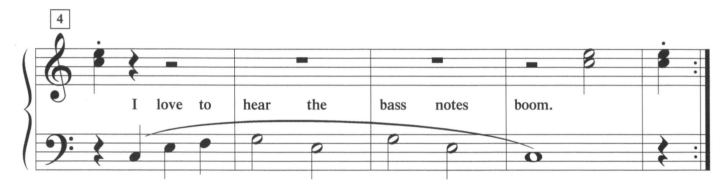

DAY 2: When the Saints Go Marching In

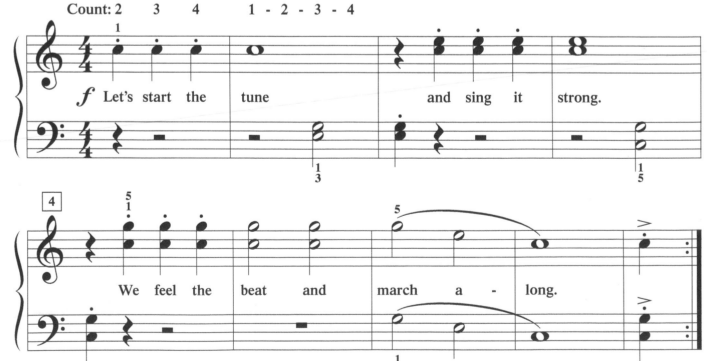

DAY 3: When the Saints Go Marching In

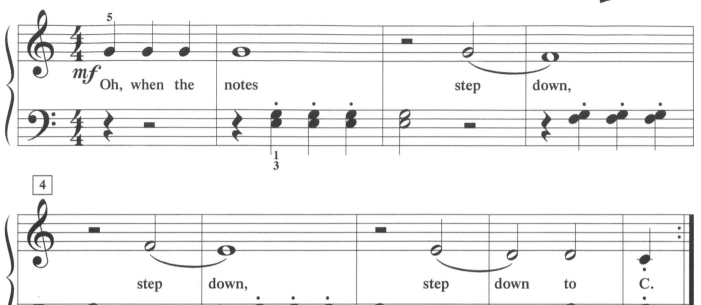

DAY 4: When the Saints Go Marching In

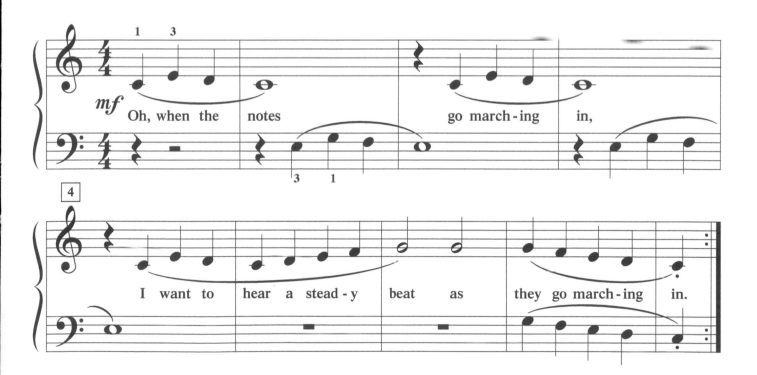

DAY 5: When the Saints Go Marching In

DON'T PRACTICE THIS!

DAY 1: Chinese Dragon

Prepare your right foot on the damper pedal.

DAY 2: Chinese Dragon

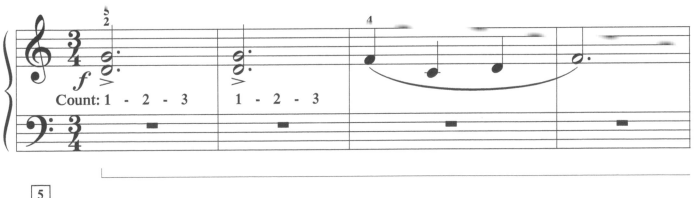

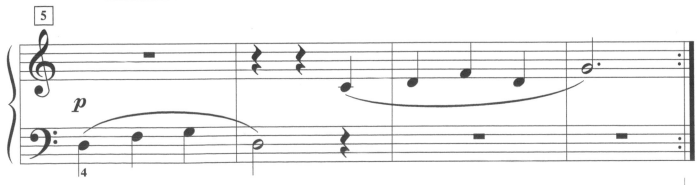

DAY 3: Chinese Dragon

Notice the time signature change.
Remember to prepare the L.H. before starting.

DAY 4: Chinese Dragon

Notice the $\frac{4}{4}$ time signature!

DAY 5: Chinese Dragon

Notice the $\frac{3}{4}$ time signature!

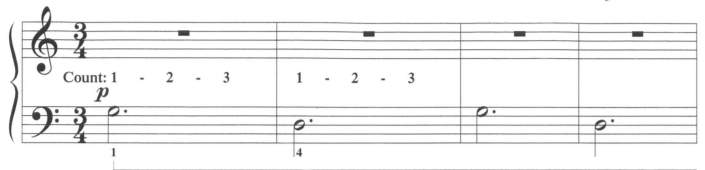

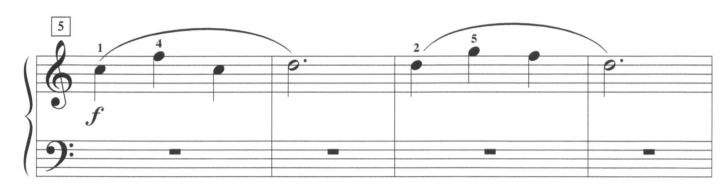

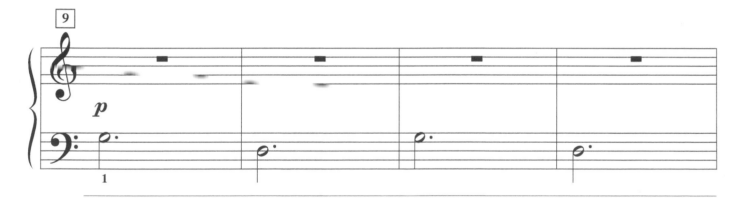

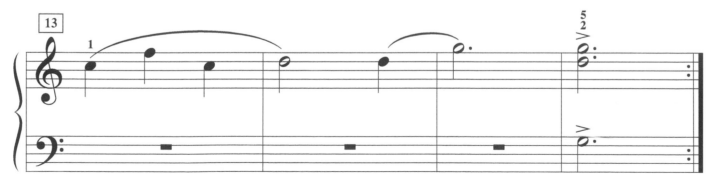

DAY 1: Forest Drums

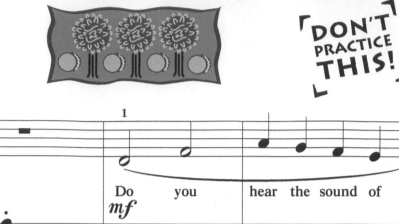

Notice the position for each hand.

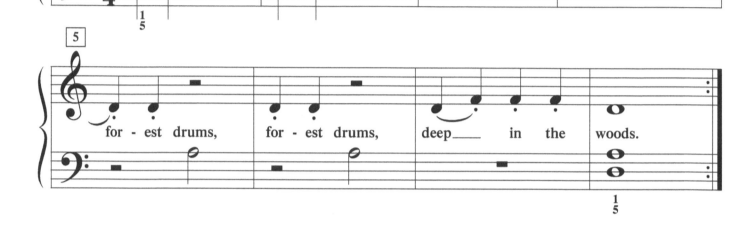

DAY 2: Forest Drums

(for L.H. alone)

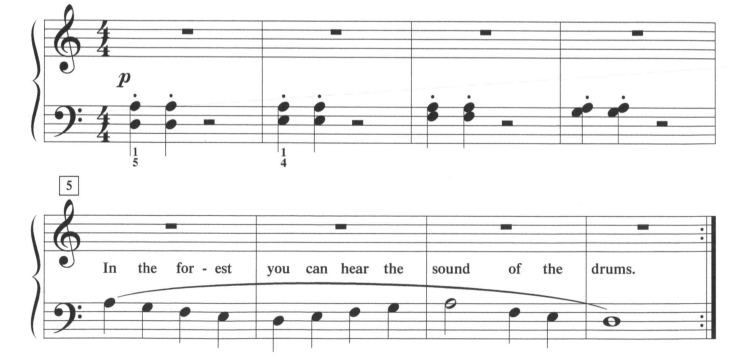

DAY 3: Forest Drums

Prepare the L.H. before starting.

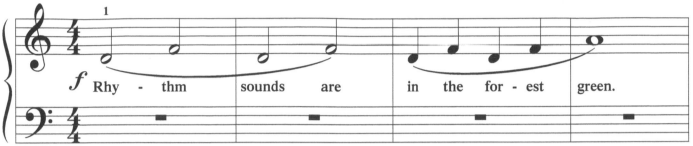

Rhy - thm sounds are in the for - est green.

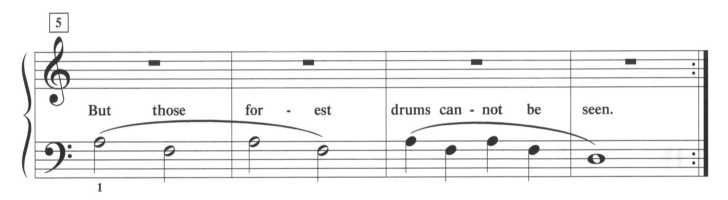

But those for - est drums can - not be seen.

DAY 4: Forest Drums

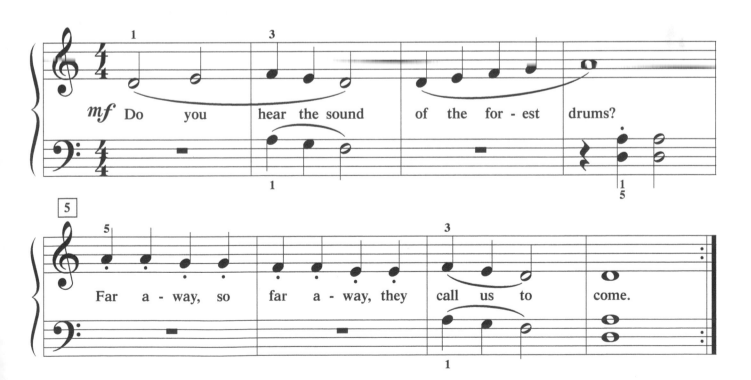

Do you hear the sound of the for - est drums?

Far a - way, so far a - way, they call us to come.

DAY 5: Forest Drums

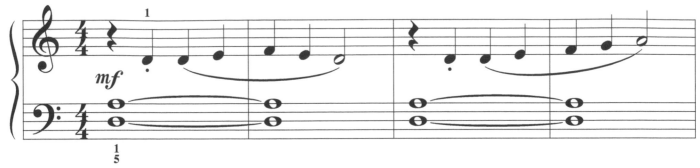

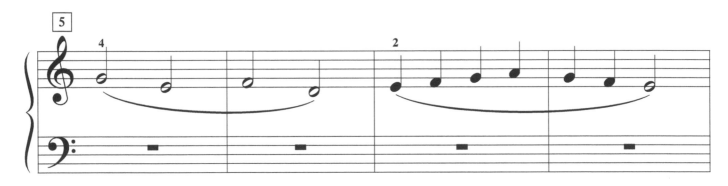

DAY 1: Pep Rally

DAY 2: Pep Rally

Where is the L.H. octave leap?

DAY 3: Pep Rally

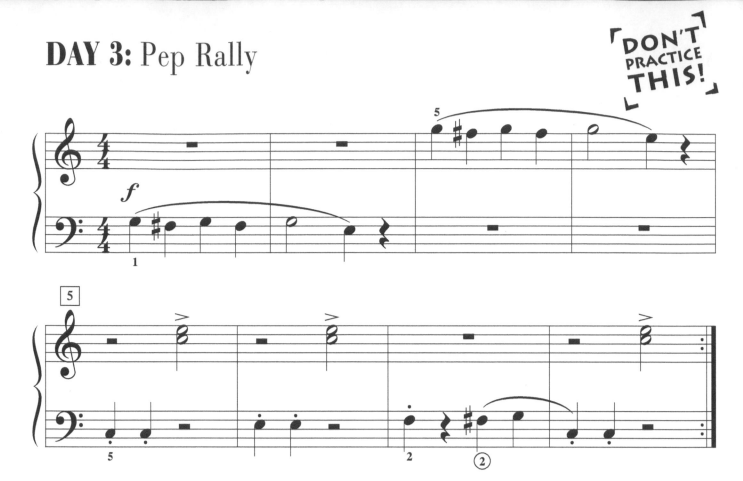

DAY 4: Pep Rally

Where is the L.H. octave leap?

DAY 5: Pep Rally

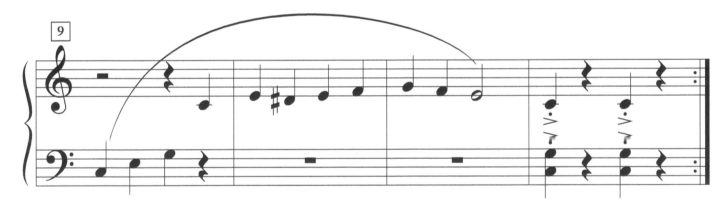

Practice naming each sharped note aloud until it's easy!

DAY 1: Zum Gali Gali

Prepare the R.H. before you begin.
Before starting, silently count the rhythm for measures 1-2.

DAY 2: Zum Gali Gali

Before starting, silently count the rhythm for measures 1-4.

DAY 3: Zum Gali Gali

Before starting, silently count the rhythm for measures 1-2.

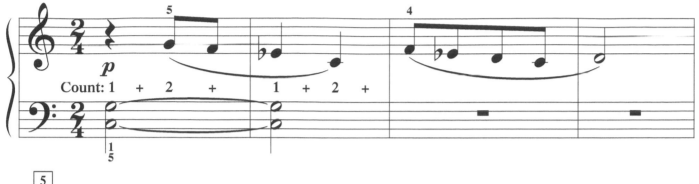

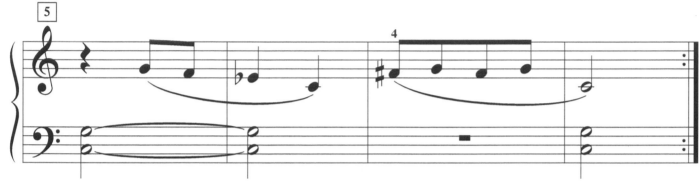

DAY 4: Zum Gali Gali

Before starting, silently count the rhythm for measures 1-4.

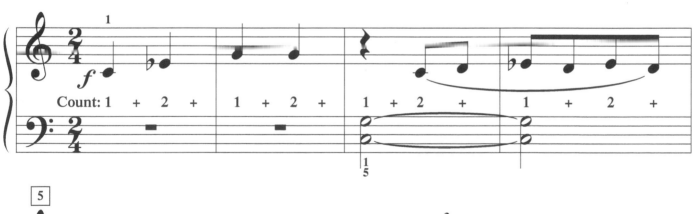

DAY 5: Zum Gali Gali

Before starting, silently count the rhythm for measures 1-4. (Count "1 + 2 +")

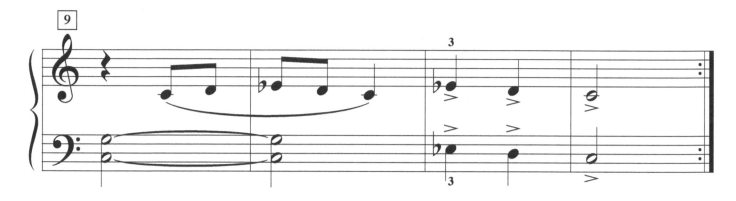

Practice naming each flatted note aloud until it's easy!

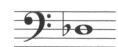

DAY 1: Sugarfoot Rag

Prepare the L.H. before starting.
Find two naturals before sightreading.

DAY 2: Sugarfoot Rag

Prepare the R.H. before starting. Notice the fingering.

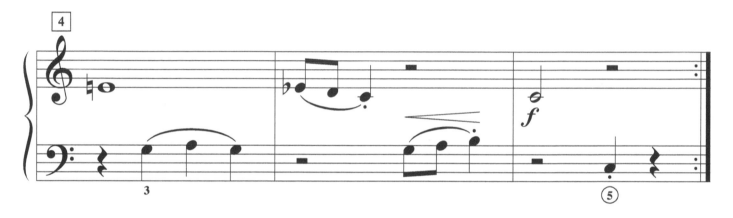

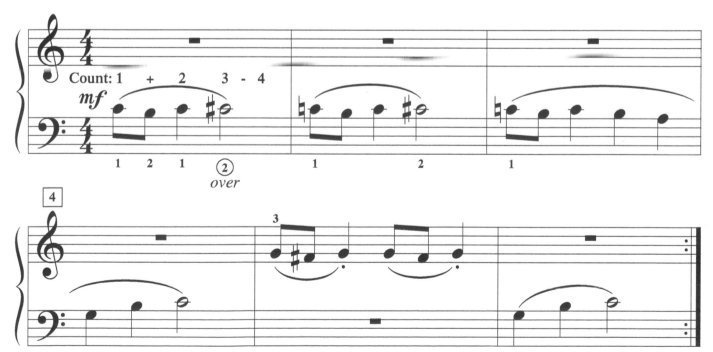

75

DAY 3: Sugarfoot Rag

Before starting, silently count the rhythm for measures 1-2.

Count: 1   +   2
3   +   4

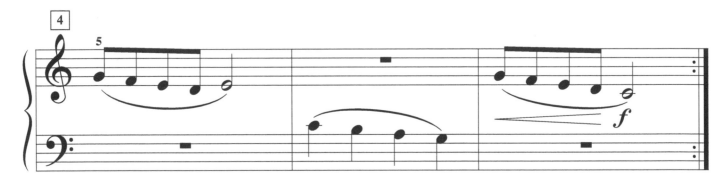

DAY 4: Sugarfoot Rag

Before starting, silently count the rhythm for measures 1-2.

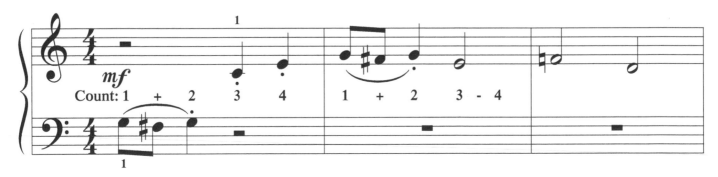

Count: 1   +   2   3   4   1   +   2   3 - 4

DAY 5: Sugarfoot Rag

Before starting, silently count the opening rhythm.
Subdivide the beat for the 8th notes.

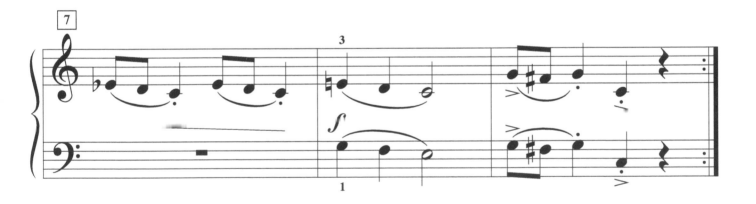

Put an X across each incorrect rhythm in 4/4 time.

DAY 1: Journey by Camel

Notice the ritardando at the end.

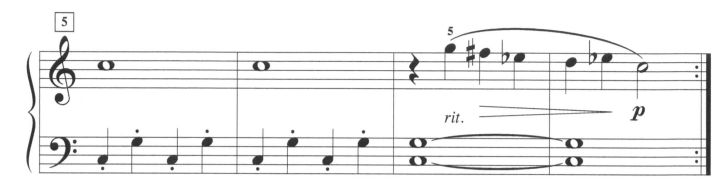

DAY 2: Journey by Camel

Notice the 8va sign at the end.

DAY 3: Journey by Camel

DAY 4: Journey by Camel

DAY 5: Journey by Camel

DAY 1: Row, Row, Row Your Boat
_____ 5-Finger Scale

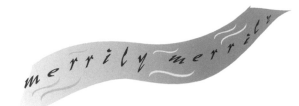

DAY 2: Row, Row, Row Your Boat
_____ 5-Finger Scale

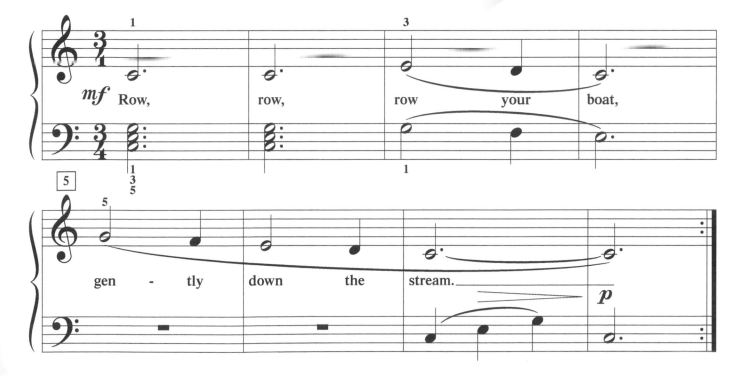

81

DAY 3: Row, Row, Row Your Boat

_____ 5-Finger Scale

Notice the L.H. crossover at the end.

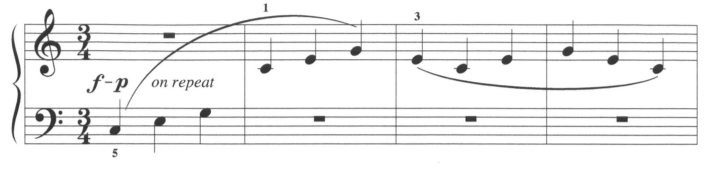

DAY 4: Row, Row, Row Your Boat

_____ 5-Finger Scale

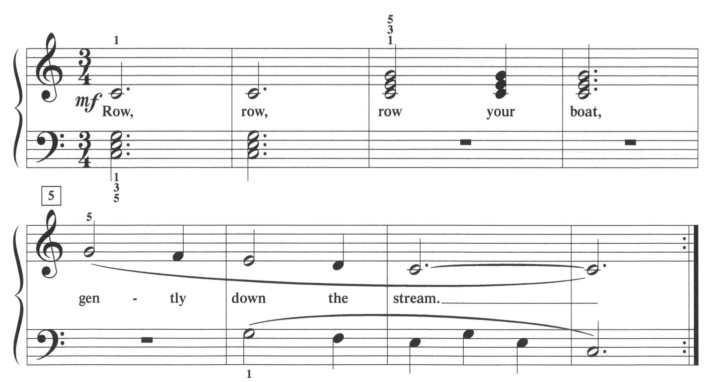

SIGHTREADING

DAY 5: Row, Row, Row Your Boat

_____ 5-Finger Scale

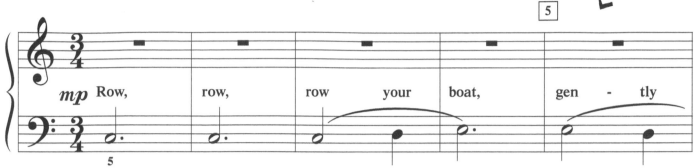

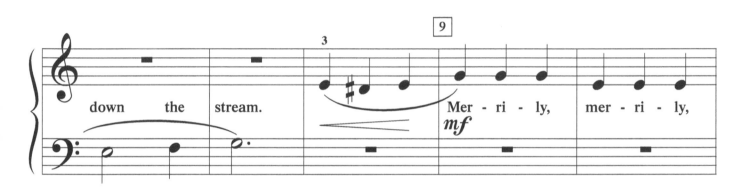

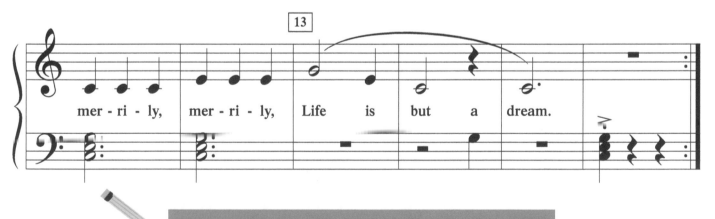

Circle all the C chords, blocked or broken. (There are 4.)

DAY 1: Prince of Denmark's March
Key of C

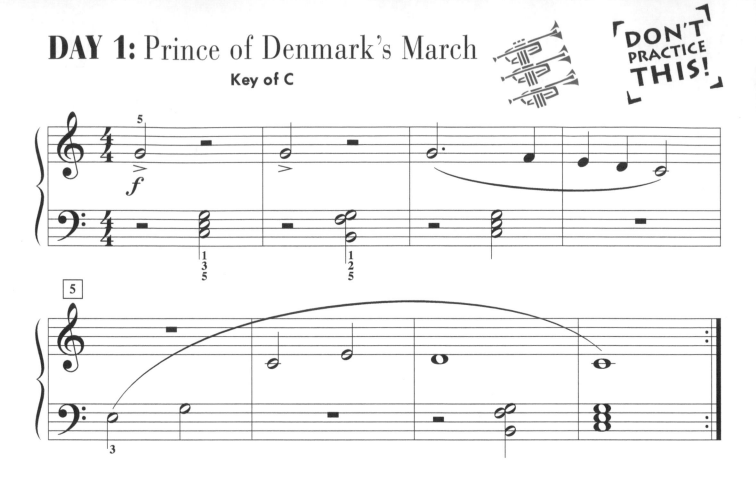

DAY 2: Prince of Denmark's March
Key of C

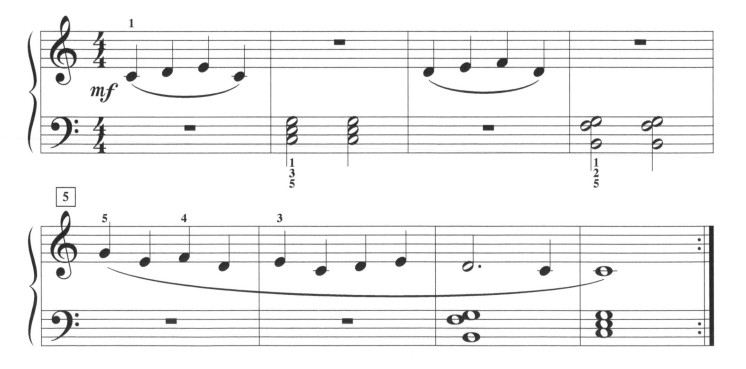

DON'T PRACTICE THIS!

DAY 3: Prince of Denmark's March

Key of C
(for L.H. alone)

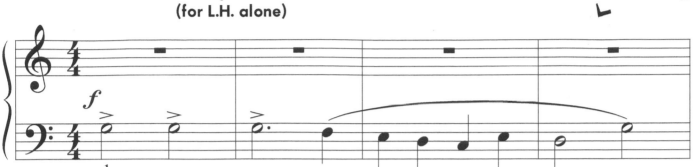

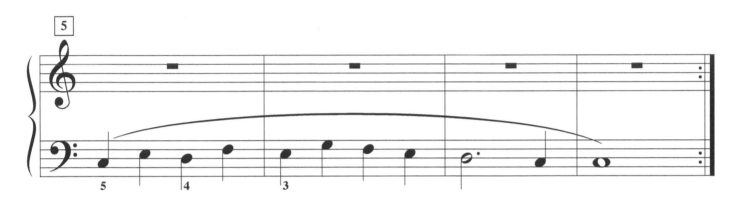

DAY 4: Prince of Denmark's March

Key of C

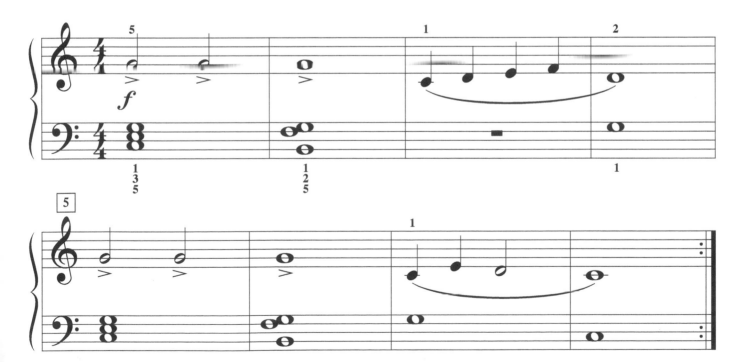

SIGHTREADING

based on Accel. Lesson Book 1, p. 83

DAY 5: Prince of Denmark's March

Key of C

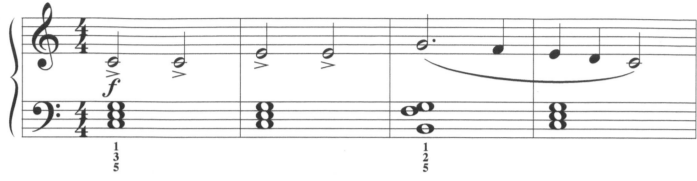

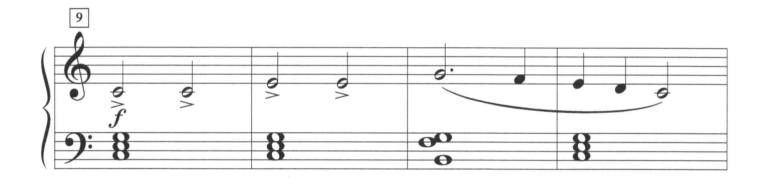

SIGHTREADING

DAY 1: Musette

_____ 5-Finger Scale

DON'T PRACTICE THIS!

DAY 2: Musette

_____ 5-Finger Scale

Prepare the L.H. before starting.
Notice the dynamic mark!

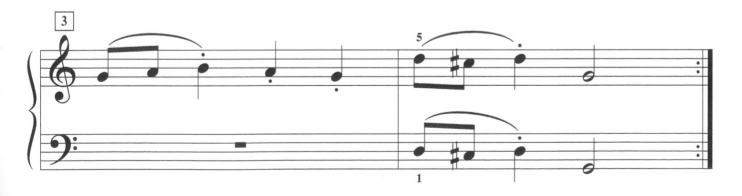

DAY 3: Musette
_____ 5-Finger Scale

DON'T PRACTICE THIS!

DAY 4: Musette
_____ 5-Finger Scale
(for L.H. alone)

DAY 5: Musette

_____ 5-Finger Scale

Practice naming each note aloud until it's easy!

DAY 1: Toccatina

Key of G

Scan the music for L.H. I and V7 chords.

DON'T
PRACTICE
THIS!

TOCCATINA

DAY 2: Toccatina

Key of G

Prepare the L.H. V7 chord before starting.

DAY 3: Toccatina
Key of G

Count: 1 + 2 +   1 + 2 +

DAY 4: Toccatina
Key of G

DAY 5: Toccatina
Key of G

DON'T PRACTICE THIS!

Create four measures of your own 2/4 rhythm.

measure   measure   measure   measure

SIGHTREADING

DAY 1: Polovtsian Dance

Key of G

Plan the rhythm of the opening measures.

DAY 2: Polovtsian Dance

Key of G

Notice the R.H. octave leap at the end.

DAY 3: Polovtsian Dance

Key of G

Plan how you will play the R.H. shift at measure 3.

DAY 4: Polovtsian Dance

Key of G

Notice the R.H. starting position.

DAY 5: Polovtsian Dance

Key of G

Notice the R.H. crossover at the end.

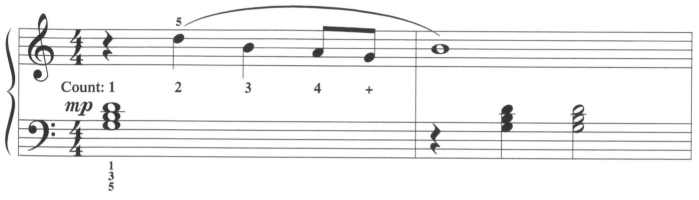

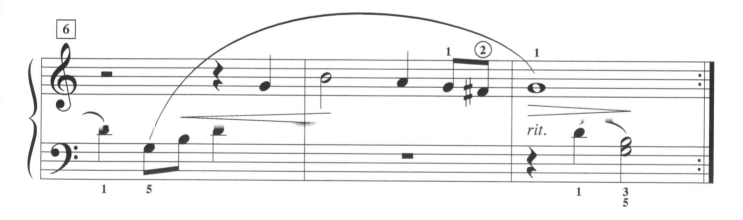

Draw bar lines for this 4/4 rhythm.

Piano Adventures® Certificate
CONGRATULATIONS

_____

(Your Name)

You are now an Accelerated Book 1 Sightreader.
Keep up the great work!

_____

Teacher

_____

Date